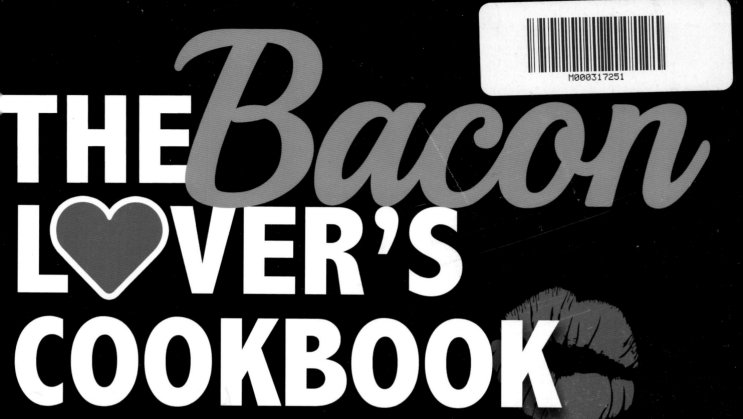

THE *Bacon* L♥VER'S COOKBOOK

THE *Bacon* L♥VER'S COOKBOOK

CHRISTINA DYMOCK

FRONT TABLE BOOKS
AN IMPRINT OF CEDAR FORT, INC.
SPRINGVILLE, UTAH

ISBN: 978-1-4621-1519-8

Published by Front Table Books, an imprint of Cedar Fort, Inc.
2373 W. 700 S., Springville, UT, 84663
Distributed by Cedar Fort, Inc., www.cedarfort.com

Library of Congress Control Number: 2014942601

Cover and page design by Bekah Claussen
Cover design © 2014 by Lyle Mortimer
Edited by Rachel Munk

Printed in the United States of America

10 9 8 7 6 5 4 3 2 1

To Craig, my guy who brings home the bacon.

Thanks for all you do—you are amazing!

CONTENTS

INTRODUCTION

Bacon has come a long way.

What started out as a basic meat—a filler if you will—served in the morning with a side of eggs and buttered toast has developed into an any-hour, any-day phenomenon. You can find bacon in all food categories and subcategories, from cookies to crackers and hamburgers to salads. It takes center stage at any meal, and sings as a snack in between.

Though it can stand alone, bacon is the perfect cuisine accessory. Bacon is so good that whenever someone asks, "Do you know what would go great with this?" the answer is bacon. Go ahead, serve it up with an ice cream sundae or crumble it over a side of veggies. No one will laugh you out of the kitchen. And if they do, don't feel bad; just take your bacon with you.

And don't think your obsession with bacon has to end when you leave the dining room. You can spice up the single's scene by wearing bacon perfume or cologne, improve your wardrobe with shirts and hoodies sporting bacon slogans, and even present the perfect gift in bacon-themed wrapping paper.

In short, bacon has invaded and no one's complaining.

METHODS FOR COOKING BACON

There are several different ways to cook bacon. The best way depends on what you're going to do with it. For example, if you are going to dip the bacon in chocolate, the oven method will allow the grease to drip off the bacon, will reduce shrinkage, and will provide a surface that the chocolate can easily adhere to. If you only want a couple pieces to finish off a sandwich or salad, then the microwave is always a good option.

Fry It

A cast iron skillet works wonders, but a regular frying pan will do just fine.

The key to making good bacon on the stove is to not cook it too fast. Place the bacon in a cold skillet, place the skillet on the stove, and turn the heat on to low. Once it starts to sizzle, you can slowly increase the heat to between medium-low and medium. If you go any higher than medium heat, your bacon will likely burn.

Bacon has its own grease, so there's no need to spray the pan with nonstick cooking spray or use butter when frying it.

Use tongs or a fork to flip the bacon after it has cooked enough to release some fat and slide easily in the pan. Ideally, you'll flip it 3–5 times to get an even appearance and crispness on both sides.

Drain the bacon fat from the pan between batches for crispier bacon, or leave it in the pan for chewier bacon strips. Once the bacon is cooked to your preferred level of crispness, use the tongs to move it to a paper bag or a plate covered in paper towels. The paper bag or towels will help absorb the grease.

Bake It

If you have a lot of bacon to make, or if you just want to keep your stovetop splatter-free, then baking it in the oven is the perfect solution.

Line a cookie sheet with aluminum foil. Place the bacon on the foil. Preheat the oven to 400 degrees and cook the bacon for 15–20 minutes, flipping it once.

If you like crispy bacon, you can line your pan with foil, place a metal rack on the pan, and then place your bacon on the rack to cook. You do not have to flip the bacon when you use a rack. Use tongs to transfer the bacon to a paper towel-lined plate.

Broil It

This one is slightly faster than other methods and it can also keep your cooktop clean.

Place the bacon on a foil-lined cookie sheet as if you were going to bake it. Move your oven rack to the top slot and turn your broiler on low. Place the cookie sheet on the top rack. Cook it for 5–7 minutes, flip the bacon over using tongs, and cook for another 5–10 minutes. Transfer the bacon to a plate covered in paper towels to drain.

Microwave It

This method is great if you are in a hurry and only need a few slices of bacon, since most microwaves will not hold a full package of bacon, or if you want to keep your stovetop clean.

Line a microwave-safe plate or dish with a double layer of paper towels. The more fatty the bacon, the more paper towels you'll want to put on the bottom layer.

Add your bacon in a single layer and then top with at least two more paper towels. Cook on high for 1 minute per slice of bacon. Check to see if the bacon is cooked through. If you'd like it crispier, cook it at 30 second intervals until the bacon is just underdone. Remove the dish from the microwave and transfer the bacon to a plate so it doesn't stick to the paper towels. It will crisp just a little more as it cools.

Iron It

The waffle iron is a great way to make bacon because it cooks both sides at the same time—no flipping necessary!

Place your waffle iron on a cookie sheet with high sides that can catch the grease as it drains away.

Preheat your waffle iron. Cut the bacon in half and simply lay the strips across the iron. Check back in 4 minutes. If the bacon isn't done, cook it in 1 minute increments until it's where you want it. Once the bacon is cooked, transfer it to a plate covered in paper towels.

Barbeque It

To barbecue bacon, place the slices on the grill. They will stick to the metal until they release enough grease to slide off. At that point, you can flip them over.

While many people swear that bacon from the barbeque is better, because of bacon's high fat content there is a real danger of starting a grease fire. For that reason, it's best to do a test piece and have a fire extinguisher at the ready. Also, don't leave your bacon unattended on the barbeque.

The alternative to placing the bacon on the grill is to make a square plate out of aluminum foil, pull up the sides to help keep the grease in, and place your bacon pieces on the aluminum foil to cook.

TIPS FOR COOKING BACON

Room Temperature

Meat and fat don't always cook at the same speed. That's why bacon tends to rumple up as it cooks; the moisture is escaping from the muscle faster than it does from the fat. In order to keep your bacon flat, which is especially important for sandwiches, try setting the package of bacon on the counter for 15-20 minutes before you cook it. This allows the fat to warm and therefore render faster so that the meat and the fat will cook at a more consistent rate.

Cooler Pan

Don't you just love the sizzle that happens when you drop a piece of bacon onto a hot pan? It can bring a smile to your face, but it's also likely to burn your bacon. If you start with a cooler pan, the fat and the meat will cook at a steady rate. Once the fat is translucent, you're pretty close to the perfect piece of bacon.

Crispy Bacon

Does your bacon come out floppy? It could be that you are putting too many pieces of bacon in the pan at one time. When they are all scrunched together, the evaporating liquids steam the bacon instead of allowing it to fry and this makes for floppy bacon.

Likewise, you'll want to make sure you keep it in a single layer. Bacon doesn't cook well when it's on top of other bacon.

OTHER BACON KNOW-HOW

- Uncooked bacon can store for a long time in the fridge so you can buy it well in advance. Always check the expiration dates and throw it out if the dates have expired or if it smells "off."

- You can store cooked bacon in the fridge for up to 7 days. This is especially advantageous if you're planning a big family breakfast. Simply reheat the bacon in the oven or microwave before serving.

- If you find a good deal on bacon, go ahead and buy a few packages. You can store bacon in the freezer for up to a month.

- Never thaw bacon in the microwave. Instead, place the package of bacon on a plate and put it in the fridge a day or two in advance.

- Never put bacon grease down your sink! It may look clear and runny when it goes in, but when the grease hits cold pipes it will quickly solidify and clog your drain. Instead, pour it into a bowl and place it in the fridge. Once the grease hardens, you can scrape it out with a spatula and throw it away. However, there are hundreds of uses for bacon grease so you may want to hang on to it to rub on the outside of potatoes before you bake them, use in a skillet to fry an egg, or grease your corn bread pan.

BREAKFAST

APPLESAUCE BACON DIPPERS

Serves 6

These freeze really well, so feel free to double the recipe on a Saturday morning and stash a few in the freezer for a quick breakfast during the week. Simply place them on a plate and heat in the microwave on high for 1–2 minutes.

1. Stir together the flour, oats, brown sugar, baking powder, and cinnamon in a medium-sized bowl. Add the vanilla, butter, milk, and applesauce. Stir well. The batter will be semi-lumpy.

2. Heat a skillet to medium-low. Spray the skillet with nonstick cooking spray or grease with butter or bacon fat. Place a small amount of batter on the skillet and then immediately set a piece of bacon in the batter. For smaller dippers, cut the bacon in half and make longer pancakes rather than round ones.

3. Once the bubbles start to form on the top of the batter, you can flip the pancake over and cook the other side. When they are cooked through, remove the pancakes from the pan. Serve with your favorite toppings.

2 cups flour

½ cup quick oats

¼ cup brown sugar

2 Tbsp. baking powder

1 tsp. cinnamon

1 tsp. vanilla

1 Tbsp. butter, melted

1 cup milk

½ cup applesauce

1 (12-oz.) pkg. bacon, cooked

INSIDE-OUT EGG MUFFINS

Serves 6

While you could cook the eggs, bacon, and toast separately, and then build a sandwich, these muffins take all the beloved flavors of a traditional egg sandwich and cut your prep time in half.

1. Preheat the oven to 400 degrees. Spray a muffin tin with nonstick cooking spray and set aside.

2. In a small mixing bowl, beat the eggs. Set aside.

3. Use a 2-inch round cookie cutter to make 12 circles out of the bread. Set aside.

4. Cut the bacon strips in half. Lay two ½-size pieces of bacon across each muffin hole in the muffin tin. They should make an X. Place a piece of bread on top of each bacon X, pressing down so the bacon and bread go all the way to the bottom of the slot. Divide the eggs between the muffin tins and sprinkle with cheddar cheese. Fold the edges of the bacon over the eggs. Bake for 20 minutes, or until eggs are cooked through.

6 eggs

6 slices bread

1 (12-oz.) pkg. hickory smoked bacon

½ cup cheddar cheese

BREAKFAST BOWLS

Serves 6

These breakfast bowls are an easy way to impress your guests. They look much harder to make than they are, and they taste amazing.

1. Preheat the oven to 400 degrees. Grease a small jelly roll pan and set aside.

2. Cut the tops off the dinner rolls and scoop out the insides, creating a bowl. Be careful not to tear a hole in the crust. Set aside.

3. In a small mixing bowl, beat together the eggs, milk, pepper, and Tabasco sauce. Add the kale, mushrooms, red pepper, and bacon. Stir well.

4. Use the batter to fill the rolls ⅔ full. Bake for 20 minutes, or until the eggs are cooked through.

6 dinner rolls

3 eggs

2 Tbsp. milk

pinch of pepper

½ tsp. Tabasco sauce

¼ cup chopped kale

¼ cup chopped mushrooms

¼ cup chopped red pepper

6 slices bacon, chopped

BACON STICKY BUNS

The combination of brown sugar and bacon has been around for ages, but never has it tasted so good as when it's all rolled up in a sticky bun. You should serve them warm, but if you've made them ahead of time, feel free to drop a patty of butter on the top and re-heat them for 30 seconds to a minute in the microwave.

FOR ROLLS

1. In a standing mixer fitted with a bread hook, stir together 2 cups of flour, sugar, and salt.

2. In a small bowl, add the yeast to the water and wait for theyeast to activate. You'll know it's ready when bubbles start to form. Pour the yeast, milk, and butter into the flour mixture and stir until smooth. Add 1½ cups of flour. If the dough is too sticky and won't come together, add another ¼ cup of flour and then check again. If needed, add the final ¼ cup of flour.

3. Grease a large mixing bowl and drop the dough inside. Flip it over once to coat. Cover the bowl with a damp towel and allow it to rise for 1 hour or until the dough doubles in size.

4. Once the dough has risen, roll it out on a lightly floured surface. Spread the ¼ cup of softened butter over the dough and then sprinkle with cinnamon. Roll the dough, starting with the longest side.

5. Spray a 9 × 13 pan with nonstick cooking spray. For the filling: In a small mixing bowl, combine the melted butter, corn syrup, molasses, cinnamon, and nutmeg. Pour it into the prepared pan. Sprinkle the brown sugar and bacon over the molasses mixture.

6. Now you can cut your rolled dough into 12 pieces and space them evenly in the pan. Cover with a damp cloth and allow to rise for 30 minutes.

7. Preheat the oven to 350 degrees. Bake rolls for 35–30 minutes or until lightly browned. Invert the pan onto a serving platter or bread board to serve.

FOR ROLLS

3½–4 cups flour, divided

½ cup sugar

1 tsp. salt

¼ cup warm water

2 Tbsp. yeast

1 cup milk, warm

⅓ cup butter, softened

FOR FILLING

¼ cup butter, softened

1 Tbsp. cinnamon

FOR TOPPING

2 Tbsp. butter, melted

¼ cup dark brown corn syrup

2 Tbsp. molasses

1 tsp. cinnamon

¼ tsp. nutmeg

¼ cup brown sugar

1 cup chopped bacon

WAFFLE SANDWICH

This is a great make-ahead recipe. The waffle recipe will make 6 large waffles, so feel free to freeze them by twos in zip-top baggies. While the recipe calls for syrup as a topping, if you'd like to make this sandwich to-go, you can use ketchup on the eggs with a dash of pepper, wrap the whole thing in a paper towel, and head out the door.

FOR THE WAFFLES

1. Preheat your waffle iron.
2. In a medium-sized mixing bowl, combine the flour, oats, baking powder, and brown sugar. Add the eggs, milk, and oil, and stir until just combined. When the waffle iron is ready, pour ⅓–½ cup of batter in and close the lid. When the iron says it's done, remove the waffle and set it aside. Repeat with remaining batter.

FOR THE SANDWICH

1. Layer one waffle, then the bacon, eggs, ham, and the other waffle. Drizzle with syrup if desired.

 **BACON BITS**

Why salt? You may wonder why they use salt to cure bacon. Salt will absorb the moisture that bacteria, mold, and other harmful microbes need to survive. In essence, it starves them to death. Soaking the bacon in brine made from salt not only makes it taste great, but the salt preserves it as well.

FOR WAFFLES

2 cups flour

½ cup quick oats

4 tsp. baking powder

1 Tbsp. brown sugar

2 eggs

1¾ cups milk

½ cup oil

FOR SANDWICH

2 waffles

2 eggs, fried

4 slices bacon, cooked

2 slices ham, fried

syrup (optional)

BACON GRAVY BREAKFAST SANDWICH

Serves 1

While the recipe says it serves one, that's if you're feeding a 15 to 17-year-old male. If you're not a bottomless pit, then it will serve two. Simply divide the ingredients between two plates.

FOR THE HASH BROWNS

1. In a small skillet, melt the butter over medium heat. Add the hash browns and sprinkle with pepper. Cook, stirring occasionally, until the hash browns are cooked through and golden brown.

FOR THE GRAVY

1. In a small saucepan, melt the bacon fat and butter over medium heat. Add the onion and cook until the onion turns brown. Discard the onion. Add the flour to the butter mixture and whisk until the flour turns brown. Whisk in the pepper, beef broth, and bacon.

FOR THE SANDWICH

1. Place the toast on a plate. Place four slices of bacon on the bread going one direction, and then place the remaining slices going the other direction. Place the hash browns on top, and then pour the gravy over the whole thing and serve.

 **BACON BITS**

Have you ever wished you could put bacon on everything? Now you can. Baconnaise, like mayonnaise, can be used as a spread and a dip. It has the smoky flavor of bacon but is lower in fat that traditional mayonnaise.

FOR HASH BROWNS

1 Tbsp. butter

1 cup frozen hash browns

½ tsp. pepper

FOR GRAVY

2 Tbsp. bacon fat

1 Tbsp. butter

1 thin slice onion

2½ Tbsp. flour

⅛ tsp. pepper

1 cup beef broth

1 slice bacon, cooked and chopped

FOR BREAKFAST SANDWICH

2 pieces toast

8 slices bacon, cooked

hash browns

gravy

BREAKFAST ENCHILADAS

Serves 6

When you roll the ingredients inside the shells, don't seal the ends. Instead, leave them open so that the eggs can make their way inside and fill them up.

1. Preheat the oven to 350 degrees. Spray a 9 × 13 pan with nonstick cooking spray and set aside.

2. In a medium-sized mixing bowl, beat the eggs, enchilada sauce, and milk together. Set aside.

3. Divide the bacon and 1 cup of shredded cheese between the 6 tortilla shells and add the beans, pepper, onion, or olives. Roll the tortilla, leaving the ends open. Place the tortilla in the prepared pan. Repeat with remaining tortillas. Pour the egg mixture over the top of the enchiladas. Cover and cook for 25 minutes.

4. Uncover and sprinkle with the remaining cheese. Bake for another 5 minutes or until the cheese is melted.

9 eggs

¾ cup mild enchilada sauce

3 Tbsp. milk

6 tortilla shells

1 (12-oz.) pkg. bacon, cooked

2 cups shredded cheddar cheese, divided

1 (15.5-oz.) can Pinto beans (optional)

½ red or green pepper, sliced thin (optional)

½ onion, sliced thin (optional)

1 (6-oz.) can olives, sliced (optional)

BACON FLAPJACKS

Your frying pan or griddle should be carefully wiped clean between each batch of flapjacks. If the pan is not wiped clean, the grease from the bacon and the sugars in the batter can quickly burn, causing the next flapjack to have a bitter taste.

1. In a large mixing bowl, stir together the flour, oats, sugar, brown sugar, baking powder, baking soda, and salt. Add the buttermilk, milk, butter, vanilla, and eggs. Stir until just combined. Carefully incorporate the bacon into the batter.

2. Warm your griddle to medium heat. Once it has heated up, spray it with a nonstick cooking spray and add ⅓ cup of batter to the griddle. When bubbles begin to rise to the surface of the batter and pop, use a spatula to flip the flapjack over to brown the other side.

3. When the batter is cooked through, remove the flapjack from the griddle. If necessary, use a bunched-up paper towel to carefully remove grease before starting the next flapjack. Repeat the process with the remaining batter.

4. Serve with your favorite toppings such as butter, syrup, jam, or honey.

2 cups flour

½ cup oats

2 Tbsp. sugar

1 Tbsp. brown sugar

4 tsp. baking powder

1 tsp. baking soda

1 tsp. salt

½ cup buttermilk

1½ cups milk

4 Tbsp. butter, melted

1 tsp. vanilla

2 eggs

1 (12-oz.) pkg. maple-flavored bacon, cooked and roughly chopped

LUNCH

BACON AND EGG SALAD SANDWICH

Serves 4

For a delicious lunch, hard–boiled eggs and bacon come together as the perfect hunger-fighting team. This bacon and egg salad is delicious on whole wheat bread, but it can also be eaten alone or used as a dip with crackers.

1. Chop the eggs into dime-size sections. Place the eggs in a small mixing bowl and add the bacon, onion, and celery. Set aside.

2. In another small bowl, stir together the mayonnaise, mustard, lemon juice, salt, and pepper. Pour over egg mixture and stir to coat. Spread the egg salad over four pieces of bread and use the other four pieces for tops. Serve with a pickle if desired.

6 eggs, hard-boiled
and peeled

6 slices bacon, cooked
and chopped

¼ onion, chopped

1 stalk celery, chopped

¼ cup mayonnaise

2 Tbsp. mustard

1 tsp. lemon juice

½ tsp. salt

½ tsp. pepper

8 slices bread

4 dill pickles (optional)

TOASTED BACON AND SALAMI SANDWICH

Salami, like bacon, is cured, not cooked. Perhaps that's one reason why they taste so good together.

1. Place the 4 slices of bread on a cookie sheet. Divide the salami between two slices of bread and then do the same with the bacon and Swiss cheese. Spread a generous amount of brown mustard on the remaining 2 slices of bread.

2. Move your oven rack to the top position. Turn your oven to low broil and insert the cookie sheet. Brown for 3–5 minutes, or until the cheese is melted and the bread is lightly toasted.

3. Place the mustard slices on top of the melted cheese slices, mustard side down, and cut in half to serve.

4 slices bread

10 slices Genoa Salami

8 slices hickory smoked, thick bacon, cooked

4 slices Swiss cheese

brown mustard

BACON BITS

Bacon technically isn't cooked, it's smoked. The type of wood chips used in the smoking process can affect the flavor. Applewood smoked bacon is generally sweeter than mesquite, while hickory is the traditional bacon-flavored smoke.

BACON TACO SALAD

Serves 4

Taco salads are spicy and filling. This one, featuring bacon, has an extra smoky flavor that's sure to delight the bacon lover in everyone.

1. Drain and rinse the beans. Place them in a small mixing bowl and add the taco seasoning. Stir to coat and set aside.

2. Shred the lettuce and place in a large salad bowl. Add the red pepper, onion, tomato, avocado, and cilantro, and then toss together. Top with the black beans, bacon, and tortilla strips. Serve with tomatillo dressing or your favorite salad dressing.

1 (15.5-oz.) can black beans

1 tsp. taco flavoring

1 head romaine lettuce

1 red pepper, chopped

½ red onion, chopped

1 tomato, sliced thin

1 avocado, sliced

½ cup cilantro

1 (12-oz.) pkg. bacon, cooked

1½ cups chipotle cheddar-flavored tortilla strips

tomatillo dressing (optional)

BACON BRUSCHETTA

Bruschetta is perfect for lunch because it's a finger food. Also, it doesn't take long to put together or cook, so you can make it and eat it in an average lunch break.

1. Slice the bread into 1 inch-thick slices and set aside.

2. Fry the bacon in a large frying pan over medium-low heat until crispy. Set the bacon on a plate covered in paper towelse to drain.

3. Pour the fat out of the frying pan and into a metal bowl. Wipe the pan out with a paper towel and put 2 teaspoons of bacon fat back in the pan. Turn the heat up to medium and place several slices of bread in the pan. Toast them on one side. Once they are done, set them on a serving plate and set aside.

4. Chop the tomatoes and place them in a medium-sized mixing bowl. Add the basil, feta cheese, garlic, balsamic dressing, and pepper. Chop the bacon into dime-size pieces and add to the tomato mixture.

5. Spoon the tomato mixture over the pieces of toasted bread and serve.

1 loaf crusty bread

8 slices bacon

8 Roma tomatoes

⅓ cup chopped fresh basil

¼ cup feta cheese

2 cloves garlic, minced

2 Tbsp. balsamic dressing

¼ tsp. pepper

BACON DOG

Serves 6

There are few things that say "guy food" like hot dogs and bacon. Because these are broiled, they can be served for the big game without having to freeze your toes off while standing over the outdoor grill.

1. Make a slit down the length of each hot dog and insert a piece of cheese in the slit. Wrap the hot dog with bacon—it will take two slices of bacon per hot dog.

2. Place the hot dogs on a metal cooking rack and place the rack on a jelly roll pan. Move your oven rack to the center position and broil the hot dogs on high for 40 minutes, turning them once after they've cooked halfway.

3. While the hot dogs are cooking, melt the butter over medium-low heat. Add the Worcestershire sauce, onion, and red pepper. Sauté until the onions are clear and the pepper is soft.

4. Divide the onions and peppers between 6 hot dog buns. Place one bacon dog on each bun, and then top with spicy mustard if desired.

6 hot dogs, bun size

12 slices applewood smoked bacon

4 oz. mozzarella cheese, cut into 6 slices

2 Tbsp. butter

1 Tbsp. Worcestershire sauce

1 yellow onion, sliced thin

1 red pepper, sliced thin

spicy mustard (optional)

 **BACON BITS**

Bacon goes beyond breakfast (and lunch and dinner). Bacon lovers no longer need to restrict their bacon obsession to a plate. You can find bacon flavored gumballs, jelly beans, and even mints, online and in specialty stores. For the especially addicted, there's also bacon-flavored dental floss.

CHICKEN BACON SALAD SANDWICH

Serves 6

The apples help this salad feel and taste light, even though it's quite filling. If you don't have an apple on hand, feel free to substitute a cup of chopped green grapes.

1. Place the apples in a medium-sized mixing bowl and sprinkle with the lemon juice. Stir around so that the lemon juice coats the apples. Add the chicken, celery, and bacon. Stir together and set aside.

2. In a small bowl, combine the Miracle Whip, mustard, garlic powder, and pepper. Whisk together and then pour over the bacon mixture and stir to coat.

3. Cut the French bread into 12 slices. Spread the bacon salad over six slices of bread. Use the remaining pieces of bread as tops to the sandwiches and serve.

1 red delicious apple, cored and chopped

1 tsp. lemon juice

1 (12.5-oz.) can chicken

1 celery stalk, chopped

4 slices bacon, cooked and chopped

½ cup Miracle Whip

1 Tbsp. spicy mustard

¼ tsp. garlic powder

¼ tsp. pepper

1 loaf French bread

 **BACON BITS**

Though the original date of creation is lost, it is said that the Chinese cured pork bellies as early as 1500 BC.

CAN'T HELP FALLING IN LOVE WITH BACON SANDWICH

Serves 2

The sweetness of caramelized bananas, combined with the salty bacon strips, are the key to this hunka hunka burnin' bacon love.

2 Tbsp. butter

1 Tbsp. brown sugar

1 banana

4 slices bread

4 Tbsp. peanut butter

8 slices bacon, cooked

1. Melt the butter in a frying pan over medium-low heat. Add the brown sugar and stir to combine.

2. Cut the banana in half and then cut each half into 4 strips. Cook the banana strips in the butter mixture for 5 minutes, flipping once.

3. While the bananas are cooking, spread 1 tablespoon of peanut butter on each slice of bread. Cut the bacon in half lengthwise and layer half on one piece of bread and half on another.

4. When the bananas are done, layer them on top of the bacon. Place the remaining two pieces of bread on top of the bananas.

5. Use a spatula to transfer the sandwiches to the pan. There should still be some sugar and butter in the pan. Cook for 3–4 minutes on each side.

 **BACON BITS**

Eating bacon while you're pregnant may increase your baby's memory capacity. Researchers at the University of North Carolina found that choline, a nutrient found in bacon, plays a critical role in the development of memory in growing babies.

GIANT COBB SANDWICH

If blue cheese and bacon aren't BFFs, then they should be. Often found together on burgers, these two also create a party of flavor in this salad.

1. Cut the loaf of bread in half lengthwise. Pull out the bread in the bottom half of the loaf and discard. Fill the hole with lettuce and blue cheese.

2. Next, layer the bacon, eggs, tomatoes, chicken, avocado, and blue cheese dressing. Place the top of the bread on the sandwich. Slice into 6 servings.

 **BACON BITS**

Bacon Day, like Easter, is a floating holiday. It's celebrated on the Saturday before Labor Day. In 2015 it will be held on September 5th.

1 loaf French bread

2 cups chopped iceberg lettuce

2 oz. blue cheese, crumbled

6 strips bacon, cooked

3 eggs, hardboiled and sliced

2 roma tomatoes, sliced thick

2 chicken breasts, shredded

1 avocado, sliced

⅓ cup blue cheese dressing

TURKEY BACON AVOCADO TRIPLE DECKER SANDWICH

Serves 1

The key to making a sandwich this big and not having stuff slide out the back when you take a bite is all in the layering. Follow the directions and your sandwich should stay together.

LAYER THE INGREDIENTS IN THIS ORDER:

1. 1 slice of bread, field greens, tomatoes, turkey, Miracle Whip, 1 slice of bread, provolone cheese, bacon, avocado, dijon mustard, 1 slice of bread.

 **BACON BITS**

The simple combination of bacon, lettuce, and tomato gained its popularity after supermarkets were able to offer fresh lettuce and tomatoes all year round. They are most often made with bread that is toasted on one side, and mayonnaise.

3 pieces whole grain sandwich bread

¼ cup field greens

4 slices tomato

6 slices mesquite turkey meat

2 tsp. Miracle Whip

2 slices provolone cheese

3 strips hickory smoked bacon, cooked

½ avocado, sliced

1–2 tsp. Grey Poupon dijon mustard

BACON SALAD WITH RED WINE VINAIGRETTE

Serves 4

There's a huge online debate about whether turkey bacon is real bacon. People generally fall into the "it is" or "it isn't" category, don't fall anywhere in between, and can become passionate about their bacon belief. Without getting into all that ... I'll just mention that you can substitute turkey bacon into this recipe if you wish.

FOR THE SALAD

1. Put the field greens in a large salad bowl. Sprinkle the onion, bacon, pine nuts, and craisins on top.

FOR THE DRESSING

1. Place the red wine vinegar and sugar in a bowl and whip together until the sugar is dissolved. Add the oil, garlic powder, oregano, and onion powder and whip for 4–5 minutes. Drizzle ½ cup of dressing over the salad and toss lightly to coat. Serve with the extra dressing on the side.

FOR SALAD

1 (6-oz.) bag field greens salad

¼ red onion, sliced thin

5 strips bacon, cooked and crumbled

¼ cup pine nuts

¼ cup craisins

FOR VINAIGRETTE

½ cup red wine vinegar

¼ cup sugar

½ cup olive oil

½ tsp. garlic powder

½ tsp. oregano flakes

¼ tsp. onion powder

DINNER

BACON AND BEAN SOUP

Serves 6

Kitchen shears make cutting bacon to the right size—raw or cooked—a breeze!

1. Cut the bacon into 1-inch pieces. Place the bacon in a medium-sized stock pot and add the Worcestershire sauce. Place the stock pot over medium heat and cook the bacon until brown and crispy, 15–20 minutes. Drain the fat off the bacon and spread the bacon pieces on a paper towel-lined baking sheet.

2. Put the butter in the stock pot and place it back on the heat; don't worry about rinsing it out. While the butter melts, cut the carrots into thin slices and slice the celery. Add the carrot slices, celery pieces, and garlic to the butter and stir. Cook for 5 minutes. Add the thyme, basil, oregano, and onion powder. Cook for 1 minute. Now you can add the bacon, beans, and chicken broth. If you'd like, you can reserve some of the bacon for a garnish.

3. Bring the liquid to a boil and then turn the heat down to low. Simmer for 20 minutes. Salt and pepper to taste.

1 lb. bacon

1 Tbsp. Worcestershire sauce

2 Tbsp. butter

½ cup mini carrots

2 celery ribs

3 cloves garlic, minced

¾ tsp. thyme

½ tsp. basil

1 tsp. oregano

1 tsp. onion powder

1 (15.5-oz.) can Navy beans

2 (14.5-oz.) cans chicken broth

salt and pepper to taste

BROWN SUGAR BARBECUE BACON BURGERS

Serves 4

An interesting thing happens when you put bacon, covered in brown sugar, in the frying pan. The fat from the bacon melts into the sugar and together they coat the bacon in a crispy shell. Consider yourself forewarned—this bacon preparation technique is highly addicting.

1. Spread ½ cup of the brown sugar on a cookie sheet or large plate. Place the bacon on top and then spread the remaining brown sugar over the top of the bacon. Set aside.

2. Place the hamburger patties in a shallow dish. Use ½ cup of barbecue sauce to marinate. Allow the bacon and the patties to flavor for at least 30 minutes.

3. In a large frying pan, cook the bacon over medium-low heat. The sugar may stick to the bacon, but that's okay. It will give the bacon a candied flavor.

4. When the bacon is done, transfer it to a paper bag-lined plate or plane plate. Do not use paper towels, as the sugars will stick to the towel.

5. While the bacon is cooking, preheat the barbecue to medium heat and cook the hamburgers for 7 minutes, flip, and cook for another 7 minutes or until the hamburgers are cooked through.

6. To build the burgers, place the patties on the bottom half of the buns. Divide the remaining barbecue sauce between hamburgers. Use three slices of bacon per burger. You may have to cut them into smaller lengths so that they fit on the burger. Add the top of the bun and enjoy.

12 slices bacon

1 cup brown sugar

4 hamburger patties

1 cup brown sugar-flavored barbecue sauce, divided

4 hamburger buns

 **BACON BITS**

Because bacon is resistant to food-born bacteria that can cause illnesses, bacon sandwiches are wonderful for picnics. Bacon's superpower doesn't transfer over to other items on the menu, so don't assume that it will protect the potato salad.

STEAK BITES

Serves 6

It doesn't get any easier to eat steak than to have it already cut to size. And steak doesn't get any more tempting than when it's wrapped in bacon.

1. Cut the steak into 1-inch cubes and place in a large plastic bag. Add the lime juice, oregano, cumin, garlic, salt, and pepper. Seal the bag and shake it well, coating the meat. Place in the fridge for 2 hours to marinate.

2. Soak 30–40 toothpicks in water while the meat is marinating.

3. Prepare a cookie sheet by covering it with aluminum foil. Set aside.

4. Once the meat is ready, cut the bacon slices into thirds. Wrap one piece of bacon around a piece of steak and secure with a toothpick. Lay the wrapped steak on its side on the prepared cookie sheet. Repeat with the remaining steak and bacon pieces.

5. Move your oven rack to the top position and turn the oven on to low broil. Slide in the cookie sheet. Cook steak bites for 5–7 minutes and then turn them over. Broil for another 5–7 minutes or until the steak is cooked to your preferred doneness.

1 lb. sirloin steak

2 Tbsp. lime juice

½ tsp. Italian oregano

½ tsp. cumin

1 clove garlic, minced

½ tsp. salt

½ tsp. pepper

1 (12-oz.) pkg. thin sliced hickory smoked bacon

BACON BITS

When it comes to calories, fat content, and cholesterol, bacon is lower on the risk list than hot dogs, hamburgers, or even donuts.

BACON-SMOTHERED CHICKEN

Serves 4

A delicious dinner can't get any easier than this. In less than 15 minutes you can have the chicken in the oven and the prep work done.

1. Preheat the oven to 350 degrees. Spray a 9 × 13 pan with nonstick cooking spray. Place the chicken breasts in the pan and set aside.

2. Using kitchen shears, cut the bacon into ½-inch pieces. Cook in a large sauté pan over medium-low heat. In the meantime, chop the celery, red onion, and mushrooms. When the bacon is about half done (7–10 minutes), add the chopped celery, red onion, and mushrooms to the pan. Cook for 7–10 minutes or until the celery is cooked through.

3. Add the garlic, pepper, flavor packet, and diced tomatoes. Simmer for 3 minutes. Pour the mixture over the chicken. Cover the baking pan with aluminum foil and bake for 35–40 minutes or until the chicken is cooked through.

4 chicken breasts

1 (12-oz.) pkg. bacon

3 celery stalks

¼ red onion

2 cups mushrooms

½ tsp. garlic powder

¼ tsp. pepper

1 (1.25-oz.) bacon and chive roasted potato flavor packet

1 (14.5-oz.) can diced tomatoes

SIMPLE BACON PASTA

Serves 4

You would think that with pasta and bacon combined, this meal would feel heavy, but it is actually a light dish.

1. Cook the pasta according to the package directions. While the pasta is cooking, chop the tomatoes and bacon. Drain the pasta and place it in a large serving dish.

2. Pour the olive oil over the pasta and add the garlic and basil. Toss to coat. Sprinkle the tomatoes and bacon over the top. Serve warm.

½ lb. thin spaghetti

3 Roma tomatoes

8 slices bacon, cooked

3 Tbsp. olive oil

2 cloves garlic, minced

1½ Tbsp. chopped
fresh basil

BACON LOAF

Despite how you may feel about the validity of turkey bacon's claim to the name bacon, this recipe is sure to please. The turkey loaf is wrapped around and in turkey bacon for an all-around delicious main dish.

1. Preheat the oven to 350 degrees. Prepare a large cookie sheet by lining it with aluminum foil and placing a metal rack on top. Set aside.

2. Lay a 1½-foot section of wax paper on the counter. Weave 10 slices of bacon together to create a solid sheet of bacon. It should be approximately 9 × 10 inches. Cook the remaining slices of bacon over medium-low heat and set aside.

3. In a medium-sized mixing bowl, stir together the ground turkey, Worcestershire sauce, tabasco sauce, salt, pepper, ground mustard, salsa, bread crumbs, and chopped onion. Spread the mixture into an 8 × 7 rectangle on the wax paper next to the bacon. Lay the cooked slices of bacon over the turkey mixture. Use the wax paper to roll the turkey mixture over the bacon, like you would cinnamon rolls.

4. Continue to use the wax paper to move the turkey roll onto the woven sheet of bacon and then to wrap the bacon around the turkey. Fold or tuck in any loose ends. Place the loaf on the metal rack on the prepared cookie sheet. Bake for 1 hour and 15 minutes to 1 hour and 30 minutes, or until the turkey is cooked through.

1 (12-oz.) pkg. Jennie-O turkey bacon

1 lb. Jennie-O ground turkey

1 Tbsp. Worcestershire sauce

¼ tsp. tobacco sauce

½ tsp. salt

¼ tsp. pepper

½ tsp. ground mustard

½ cup salsa

½ cup bread crumbs

½ cup chopped onion

 **BACON BITS**

In the English town of Dunmow, a thriving commercial center in the 12th century, a married man was awarded a slab of bacon if he could swear before the church that he had not fought with his wife for a year and a day. Now that's motivation for matrimonial merriment.

BACON BURGERS

Serves 4

The only way to describe these bacon burgers is to say that they are "deep on flavor." Don't rush the grilling process and never press the burger flat against the grill; you want to keep all those delicious juices inside.

1. In a small bowl, whisk together the Worcestershire sauce, lime juice, A1 sauce, paprika, cumin, black pepper, and garlic. Once combined, brush the sauce onto each side of the hamburger patties. Allow the burgers to marinate for 30 minutes.

2. Turn your barbeque to medium heat. Cook the burgers for 5–10 minutes or until they are cooked through.

3. Build your burger with the bottom of the bun, lettuce, tomato, cooked hamburger patty, bacon, and then the top of the bun.

2 Tbsp. Worcestershire sauce

1 tsp. lime juice

2 Tbsp. A1 sauce

¼ tsp. paprika

1 tsp. cumin

1 tsp. black pepper

1 tsp. garlic sauce

4 hamburger patties

8 slices bacon, cooked

4 hamburger buns

lettuce

tomato

 **BACON BITS**

Canadian bacon is not really bacon, even though it is often called "country bacon." It's a fully cooked, smoked pork loin that is similar to ham.

CHICKEN BACON JACK

Serves 6

If you aren't a fan of the kick-in-the-taste-buds cheese known as Monterey Jack cheese, you can substitute provolone. If you do make the substitution, use Italian bread crumbs instead of plain.

1. Preheat the oven to 425 degrees. Spray a 9 × 13 pan with nonstick cooking spray and set aside.

2. Place a chicken breast between two pieces of wax paper and pound it to ¼ inch thickness. Place a slice of cheese and two slices of bacon at one end of the chicken. Roll the bacon inside the chicken and secure the chicken with a toothpick so it doesn't unroll. Dip the rolled chicken in the milk and then in the bread crumbs, coating it well. Place the chicken in the prepared pan. Repeat with remaining chicken breasts.

3. Bake for 30–35 minutes, or until the chicken is cooked through.

6 chicken breasts

6 slices Monterey Jack cheese

12 slices bacon, cooked

1 cup milk

1½ cups bread crumbs

BACON BITS

Though not often done, bacon can be flavored at home. Simply soak the bacon in a marinade for at least 24 hours before cooking. You can make garlic bacon, brown sugar bacon, pepper bacon, and much more.

BACON-WRAPPED SHRIMP

Serves 6

Nothing can compare with nor imitate the perfect flavor combination that comes together when you wrap shrimp in bacon. Be prepared to fall deeply in love.

1. Place a large skillet on the stove and turn the heat to medium-low.

2. Cut each strip of bacon into three pieces. Wrap a cut piece of bacon around one shrimp, taking the bacon under the bow and twisting it inside the C. Lay the shrimp on its side in the skillet. Repeat with remaining shrimp and bacon.

3. Cook for 3½ minutes. Use tongs to flip the shrimp to the other side. Cook for another 3–4 minutes. If needed, turn once more for another 3 minutes. Remove the shrimp from the skillet and place on a paper towel to drain the grease. Serve hot with a side of blue cheese dressing for dipping if desired.

1 (12-oz.) pkg. large shrimp, precooked

1 (12-oz.) pkg. hickory smoked bacon

blue cheese dressing (optional)

 **BACON BITS**

For those who love bacon and want to share that love, the Blue Ribbon Bacon Festival—or Baconfest—is held every year in Iowa. Those who attend can meet the Bacon Queen, enter the bacon eating contest, attend lectures, peruse the booths, and shop for all things bacon. If you'd like to attend, you'd better plan in advance as tickets usually sell out months in advance.

CHICKEN BACON RANCH PIZZA

Serves 6

This recipe makes one large pizza from scratch, but you can use store-bought crusts to speed up the process if you'd like.

FOR SAUCE

1. Melt the butter in a small saucepan over low heat. Add the cream cheese and stir until melted. Add the cream, garlic, and Italian seasoning, and whisk together until the mixture starts to boil. Add the flour, salt, and pepper, and boil for 2 minutes. Remove from heat and set aside while you make the crust.

FOR CRUST

1. In a small bowl, stir together the yeast and water. Let it sit for about 10 minutes to activate the yeast. If your yeast isn't growing, try sprinkling a pinch of sugar in with it. Stir in the sugar, flour, salt, and butter until the dough is smooth. Let it sit for 5 minutes. Roll the dough into the desired shape on a lightly floured countertop. Transfer it to a pizza pan or stone that has been dusted with corn flour.

FOR THE PIZZA

1. Preheat the oven to 450 degrees. (Or follow the instructions on the pre-made pizza crust package.) Spread the ranch dressing and sauce over the dough. Sprinkle half the mozzarella cheese on the sauce, and then add the chicken, bacon, onion, and remaining cheese.

2. Bake for 15–20 minutes, or until the pizza crust is golden brown and the cheese is melted. Or follow the baking instructions listed on the pizza crust package.

FOR SAUCE

¼ cup butter

1 oz. cream cheese

½ cup heavy cream

3 cloves garlic, minced

½ tsp. Italian seasoning

1 tsp. flour

dash of salt and pepper

FOR THE CRUST

2½ tsp. yeast

1 cup warm water

1 tsp. sugar

2½ cups flour

1 tsp. salt

2 Tbsp. butter, melted

FOR PIZZA

⅓ cup ranch dressing

1½ cups chopped chicken

6 slices bacon, cooked and chopped

¼ cup chopped red onion

1½ cups shredded mozzarella cheese

BARBARIAN BACON SKEWERS

Serves 6

This is a household favorite. Once you get the hang of securing the bacon and chicken to the skewer, they come together fast. When you try them, you'll want to make them again and again.

3 Tbsp. flour

½ tsp. pepper

1 tsp. rosemary

6 chicken tenders

6 slices bacon, medium thickness

1. Soak 6 skewers in water for an hour. Once they are ready, preheat the oven to 400 degrees.

2. Line a cookie sheet or large jelly roll pan with aluminum foil to catch the bacon grease as the meat cooks. Place a metal cooking rack on the pan to keep the meat out of the fat as it cooks and make the bacon crispy instead of soft.

3. Place the flour, pepper, and rosemary on a flat plate. Use a fork to gently combine the ingredients.

4. Rinse a chicken tender and roll it in the flour mixture. Then, lay a piece of bacon on your work surface and line the chicken tender up with the end of the bacon. Spear that end of the bacon and chicken with a skewer and then push the skewer in and out, securing both the chicken and the bacon to the stick. Wrap the tail end of the bacon around the chicken and place the whole thing on the wire rack. Repeat with the remaining chicken and bacon.

5. Bake for 20 minutes. Turn the skewers over and bake for another 20 minutes. Allow to cool slightly before serving so the skewers can be handled.

 **BACON BITS**

Set the stage for a beautiful evening with your significant other using bacon scented candles and dabbing on a touch of bacon perfume. Be sure to keep some bubbly bacon soda on ice to enjoy in front of a roaring fire. Finally, you can feed each other pieces of chocolate-covered bacon. Who says bacon can't be romantic?

HONEY MUSTARD BACON DRUMSTICKS

Simple meals are a favorite of any home cook. When they come out this good, they are a favorite for the whole family.

1. Preheat the oven to 350 degrees. Spray a 9 × 13 casserole dish with nonstick cooking spray and set aside.

2. Remove the skin from the drumsticks, and then rinse and pat dry. Set aside.

3. In a small bowl, whisk together the Miracle Whip, honey, Dijon mustard, and horseradish.

4. Divide the honey mustard sauce between the drumsticks and coat each one. Then wrap a slice of bacon around each piece of chicken and place the chicken in the prepared pan. Cover the pan with aluminum foil and bake for 45 minutes. Remove the foil, drain the liquid from the pan, and bake for another 7 minutes. Turn the chicken over and finish baking for another 7 minutes, or until the bacon is cooked.

1 (32-oz.) pkg. chicken drumsticks

1 cup Miracle Whip

⅓ cup honey

3 Tbsp. Dijon mustard

1 tsp. horseradish

7–8 slices thick cut hickory smoked bacon

≋ BACON BITS

Many bacon slices get their pink color from the salt used to cure them, although some get their coloring from the liquid smoke soak they take before being cured.

SIDES

BACON AND BROCCOLI BAKE

Serves 6

This is a side dish that comes together easily and makes a good impression.

1. Preheat the oven to 350 degrees. Spray an 8 × 8 pan with nonstick cooking spray and set aside.

2. Flatten four biscuits with a rolling pin and lay them across the bottom of the pan.

3. In a medium-sized mixing bowl, combine the butter, mustard, basil, onion powder, and lemon juice. Add the cheese, broccoli, and bacon. Stir to coat. Pour the bacon mixture into the pan and spread out. Flatten the remaining biscuits and place on top of the broccoli mixture.

4. Bake for 20–25 minutes, or until biscuits are golden brown.

1 (16.3-oz.) flaky layers refrigerated biscuits tube, 8 biscuits

1 Tbsp. butter, at room temperature

2 Tbsp. spicy mustard

1 tsp. dried basil

1½ tsp. onion powder

1 tsp. lemon juice

1½ cups shredded mozzarella cheese

1½ cups broccoli, cooked

1 (12-oz.) pkg. bacon, cooked and crumbled

MOM'S BAKED BEANS

Serves 10

This recipe has always been a family favorite. Mom would make it up for get-togethers with extended family or to take to a potluck. There weren't many leftovers.

1. Cut the bacon into 1-inch pieces and cook in a skillet over medium-low heat. Remove the bacon from the pan using a slotted spoon. Remove half the bacon drippings and add the onion, peppers, and celery to the pan. Sauté until the vegetables are tender, 5–7 minutes.

2. Place the cooked vegetables, pork n' beans, ketchup, brown sugar, Worcestershire sauce, and bacon in a large slow cooker. Cover and cook on low for 5 hours.

1 (12-oz.) pkg. mesquite bacon

1 onion, chopped

2 green peppers, chopped

4 celery ribs, chopped

4 (31-oz.) cans pork n' beans

½ cup ketchup

½ cup brown sugar

1 Tbsp. Worcestershire sauce

 **BACON BITS**

Bacon is like frosting—you add it to another food to make it taste better.

TWICE-BAKED POTATOES

Though they take a little longer than a basic baked potato, the effort is worth it. If you'd like, you can brush your potatoes with bacon grease instead of olive oil for an added smoky flavor.

1. Preheat the oven to 400 degrees.

2. Wash and dry the potatoes. Brush each potato with olive oil and pierce the skin in several places with a fork. Place potatoes on the oven rack and bake for 1 hour and 15 minutes, or until the potato gives when squeezed slightly.

3. Once the potatoes are cooked through, allow them to cool until you can handle them, but don't let them get cold.

4. Cut off the top third of each potato and scrape out the insides of both the tops and the bottoms. Discard the tops.

5. In a medium-sized mixing bowl, mash the potato insides, sour cream, milk, ranch dressing, butter, 1 cup of the cheese, and bacon pieces with a potato masher.

6. Fill each potato skin with the mashed potatoes. Place the potatoes on a cookie sheet and bake at 350 degrees for 15–20 minutes, or until cooked through. Top with remaining cheese to serve.

4 large russet potatoes

1 Tbsp. olive oil

¼ cup sour cream

½ cup whole milk

¼ cup ranch dressing

3 Tbsp. butter

1½ cups cheddar cheese, divided

8 slices bacon, cooked and chopped

 **BACON BITS**

Bacon can mean so many things to so many people. It's the perfect way to say, "I love you," "I'm sorry," or "Congratulations."

BACON-WRAPPED TOMATOES

Serves 4

Wait to make your first turn until after the bacon has released enough fat to slide easily across the grill. If it sticks, you'll need to wait a minute or two more. As always, when you cook bacon on a barbecue, keep a watchful eye.

1. Presoak 18 toothpicks for one hour in a cup of water.

2. Cut a small well in the top of each tomato. Fill the well with feta cheese and set aside.

3. Cut the bacon strips in half. Wrap one piece of bacon around each tomato and secure with a toothpick.

4. Cook the bacon tomatoes at medium-high heat on the barbeque for 15–20 minutes, turning often.

18 cherry tomatoes

1 oz. feta cheese, crumbled

9 slices bacon

 **BACON BITS**

As far as gifts go, a pound of bacon is sure to be used and enjoyed. It's never returned or re-gifted and it's always appreciated.

BACON-WRAPPED JALAPENO PEPPERS

Makes 6 peppers

These bad boys are need-to-gargle-sour-cream hot. You can decrease the heat by using a different type of cheese—provolone is nice. If you're serving them to guests, be sure to have plenty of milk or bread on hand, as both can help to reduce the burn.

1. Preheat the oven to 400 degrees. Prepare a cookie sheet by lining it with aluminum foil and place a metal cooking rack over the foil. Set aside.

2. In a small bowl, beat together the cream cheese and pepper jack cheese until well combined. Set aside.

3. Cut the peppers in half lengthwise, and remove the membrane and seeds. Fill each half with the cream cheese mixture. Press the peppers back together and wrap each one with bacon. It may take two slices to go all the way down the pepper, depending on the size of your pepper.

4. Place the wrapped peppers on the metal cooking rack. Move the oven rack to the middle position. Bake the peppers for 30 minutes, turning once, or until the bacon is crisp.

4 oz. cream cheese, at room temperature

¼ cup pepper jack cheese, cubed into ¼-inch pieces

6 large jalapeno peppers

12 slices bacon

 **BACON BITS**

Unlike other foods, bacon is always in season. You can enjoy your favorite meat any time of year.

BACON ONION ARTISAN BREAD

Makes 1 Loaf

One of the best selling points for this bread is that you can make the dough the night before and allow it to set while you sleep. The next day, you can make up a fresh loaf of beautiful bread and serve it warm.

1. In a medium-sized mixing bowl, stir together the flour, salt, yeast, green onion, bacon, and Italian seasoning. Add the water and stir until the flour is incorporated and the dough forms a shaggy ball. Cover the bowl with plastic wrap and allow to rise for 8–18 hours, or until bubbles appear on the top of the dough and the dough has doubled in size.

2. Preheat the oven to 450 degrees. Place your baking pan and lid in the oven as it preheats.

3. Place the dough on a lightly floured surface. Sprinkle flour on top of the dough. Fold the edges into the center and press down. Then repeat the process, creating a ball.

4. Once the oven is heated, use heating pads to remove the pan from the oven. Place the ball of dough in the pan, cover, and bake for 30 minutes. Remove the cover and bake for 12–15 minutes more, or until the crust is a light golden brown. Remove immediately from the pan and allow to cool on a bread board.

3 cups flour

1½ tsp. salt

1 tsp. yeast

1½ Tbsp. chopped green onion

½ cup chopped bacon (about 4 slices)

½ tsp. Italian seasoning

1¾ cups water

 **BACON BITS**

Save the drippings! Bacon fat can be used to cook your favorite foods in place of butter. Use it in the frying pan to cook potato slices or grilled cheese sandwiches, melt it down to make salad dressings, or put a tablespoon in with your boiling water when you make pasta.

STUFFED MUSHROOMS

These are a great as a side dish, appetizer, or snack. They're fairly simple to make and make a big impression, so feel free to share with a friend.

1. Wash mushrooms and pat dry. Remove the stems and chop them into fine pieces.

2. In a large frying pan, melt the butter over medium heat. Add the chopped stems, onion, red pepper, celery, garlic, and bacon. Stir while cooking for 5–7 minutes or until the onions are translucent.

3. Add the bread crumbs and salt and pepper and stir well. Remove the mixture from the heat and preheat the oven to 325 degrees.

4. Line a large cookie sheet with aluminum foil and spray with nonstick cooking spray. Set aside.

5. Stuff each mushroom cap with the bread crumb mixture and then place them on the cookie sheet. Leave space between each cap. Bake for 20–25 minutes or until the mushrooms are cooked through and liquid forms at their base.

2 (14-oz.) pkg. jumbo mushrooms (or 2 dozen mushrooms)

5 Tbsp. butter

4 Tbsp. finely chopped onion

3 Tbsp. finely chopped red pepper

1 celery stalk, finely chopped

2 cloves garlic, minced

3 strips bacon, cooked and chopped

1½ cups bread crumbs

¼ tsp. salt

¼ tsp. pepper

CRAB DIP

This is a great dish for any occasion. If there are leftovers (highly unlikely), it also makes a delicious bagel sandwich.

1. In a medium-sized mixing bowl, beat together the cream cheese, lemon juice, and sour cream. Add the onions, Worcestershire sauce, horseradish spread, thyme, and pepper. Add the crab meat and bacon and gently stir in by hand. Refrigerate until ready to serve. Leftovers can be stored in a covered container in the fridge.

 **BACON BITS**

Cooked bacon can be stored in an airtight container in the fridge for up to seven days.

1 (8-oz.) pkg. cream cheese, softened

1 Tbsp. lemon juice

⅔ cup sour cream

2 green onions, chopped

1 Tbsp. Worcestershire sauce

3 Tbsp. horseradish spread

½ tsp. thyme

¼ tsp. pepper

2 (4.25-oz.) cans crab meat, drained

4 slices mesquite bacon, cooked and crumbled

SWEETS

WHITE CHOCOLATE AND BACON TREATS

Makes 16 treats

Do you have a friend who is also a bacon lover? These sweets are a wonderful way to say you care. Not only are they scrumptious, but they also package and travel well.

1. Crumble the bacon and set aside.

2. Spray an 8 × 8 pan with nonstick cooking spray and set aside.

3. In a large sauce pan, melt the butter and marshmallows over medium-low heat. Once smooth, remove from heat and add the vanilla and bacon. Quickly stir in the cereal and then transfer the mixture to the prepared pan. Spray the bottom of a metal spoon with nonstick cooking spray and use it to press the mixture into the pan. Set aside to cool.

4. In a small sauce pan, melt the white chocolate chips and shortening over low heat. Drizzle the chocolate over the treats. Allow the chocolate to set before cutting.

5 slices bacon, cooked

2 Tbsp. butter

1 (10-oz.) pkg. marshmallows

1 tsp. vanilla

4 cups crispy rice cereal

¼ cup white chocolate chips

1 tsp. shortening

BACON CANDY

Bacon. Candy. Need I say more?

1. Cook the bacon using the oven method on page xi. Allow to cool completely.
2. Melt the chocolate pieces using the double broiler method indicated on the package.
3. Place a long piece of wax paper on the counter. Break the bacon slices into thirds. Pick up a bacon slice by the long edge. Lay one side of the bacon in the chocolate and then flip it over and do the other side. Gently shake the excess chocolate off the bacon before placing it on the wax paper to set. Repeat with remaining bacon and chocolate.

1 lb. thick sliced bacon

1 (12-oz.) bag light chocolate candy melts

 **BACON BITS**

According to porkretail.org, 62% of restaurants in the United States have bacon on the menu.

JUST BACON COOKIES

Many recipes for bacon cookies also include chocolate chips. These cookies are just bacon cookies, for the bacon lover in all of us.

1. Preheat the oven to 350 degrees.
2. In a medium-sized mixing bowl, cream together the butter, sugar, and brown sugar. Add the eggs one at a time, beating between additions. Add the vanilla, salt, baking soda, and flour. Beat well. Add the bacon and stir lightly. Roll into 1-inch balls and place on an ungreased cookie sheet. Bake for 8–10 minutes, or until centers are set.

½ cup butter, at room temperature

½ cup sugar

½ cup brown sugar

2 eggs

1 tsp. vanilla

½ tsp. salt

1 tsp. baking soda

2 cups flour

12 slices bacon, cooked and chopped

 **BACON BITS**

Forty-five percent of bacon cooked at home is cooked on the stovetop.

BACON AND CARAMEL-DIPPED APPLES

Makes 6

Apples, caramel, and bacon harmonize to create a treat as beautiful as it is decadent. You can give these as gifts, or hide them away for a special treat for yourself. Either way, you'll be amazed at how easy they are to make.

1. Wash the apples under hot water to remove any wax. Remove the stems. Insert a stick into the top of each apple and set aside.

2. Pour the crumbled bacon pieces onto a plate and set aside.

3. Melt the caramels and 2 tablespoons cream in a double boiler over medium-low heat. If the caramel is too thick for dipping, add the remaining tablespoon of cream. If it is fine, then omit the last tablespoon of cream and proceed.

4. Once the caramel is smooth, add the vanilla and salt. Remove bowl from the heat and turn off the stove.

5. Holding tight to the stick, dip an apple in the caramel. You can tip the bowl to the side and spin it through to get an even coating. Tap the stick on the side of the bowl to remove excess caramel. Immediately roll the apple in the bacon. Set the apple on a piece of wax paper or flattened muffin wrapper. Place in the refrigerator to help the caramel set and not run. Repeat with remaining apples. Store in a cool, dry place for up to a week.

6 red delicious apples

12 slices bacon, cooked and crumbled

1 (11-oz.) pkg. caramels

2–3 Tbsp. heavy cream

1 tsp. vanilla

dash of salt

 **BACON BITS**

Bacon and eggs go together like, well, bacon and eggs. When there are eggs on the breakfast menu, bacon is there 71% of the time, according to porkretail.org.

ROOT BEER AND BACON CUPCAKES

This may seem like a strange combination of flavors, but the sweet root beer matches up well against the salty bacon.

FOR CUPCAKES

1. Preheat the oven to 350 degrees. Line a muffin tin with cupcake liners and set aside.

2. In a medium-sized mixing bowl, beat the eggs until frothy. Add the brown sugar, oil, vanilla, and root beer. Mix well. Add the flour, salt, baking soda, and baking powder and mix well. Stir the bacon pieces in by hand. Fill the muffin cups ¾ full. Bake for 15–18 minutes or until a toothpick inserted in the center comes out clean. Remove the cupcakes from the pan and allow to cool on a wire rack.

FOR SYRUP

1. Bring the root beer to boil in a small sauce pan over medium heat. Allow to boil for 30 minutes. Remove from heat and set aside.

FOR FROSTING

1. In a medium-sized mixing bowl, beat the shortening until fluffy. Add the salt, powdered sugar, vanilla, and 3 tablespoons of root beer syrup. Beat well. If the frosting isn't moist enough, add another tablespoon of root beer syrup and beat again. If it's still too thick, continue adding syrup until it forms the right consistency.

TO ASSEMBLE

1. Once cupcakes have cooled, use a pastry brush to distribute the remaining root beer syrup between the cupcakes by simply brushing it across the tops of the cupcakes.

2. Frost the cupcakes with the frosting and sprinkle with the bacon reserved for topping.

FOR CUPCAKES

2 eggs

½ cup brown sugar

¼ cup oil

1 tsp. vanilla

½ cup root beer

2 cups flour

¼ tsp. salt

½ tsp. baking soda

2 tsp. baking powder

4 slices applewood smoked bacon, cooked and chopped

FOR ROOT BEER SYRUP

2 cups root beer

FOR FROSTING

½ cup butter-flavored shortening

½ tsp. salt

4 cups powdered sugar

1 tsp. vanilla

4–5 Tbsp. root beer syrup

TOPPING

2 slices applewood bacon, cooked and crumbled

BACON BARS

These bars have it all—butter, almonds, caramel, chocolate, cream cheese, and of course—bacon! Don't be shy, asking for seconds is expected.

FOR THE CRUST

1. Preheat the oven to 350 degrees. Spray a 9 × 9 dish with nonstick cooking spray and set aside.

2. Melt the butter in a small, microwave-safe dish. Add the flour and almonds and mix well. Press the dough into the prepared pan and bake for 15–17 minutes or until cooked through.

3. Remove the crust from the oven and immediately spread the kisses evenly around the dough. Sprinkle the bacon on the chocolate. Allow to cool.

FOR THE CREAM FILLING

1. Whip the cream until stiff peaks form. Add the sugar and vanilla and whip again. Cut the cream cheese into 1-inch squares. Add the cream cheese to the cream and sprinkle the powdered sugar over the mixture. Whip together until smooth. Spread over the chocolate and bacon layer in the pan. Place in the fridge while preparing the chocolate topping.

FOR THE CHOCOLATE TOPPING

1. In a small saucepan, melt the chocolate chips with the butter. Add the cream and stir well. Pour over the cream filling and spread evenly. Refrigerate for 3–5 hours or until set.

CRUST

½ cup butter

1 cup flour

½ cup chopped almonds

LAYERS

20 caramel filled kisses

5 slices bacon, cooked and crumbled

CREAM FILLING

¾ cup whipping cream

1½ Tbsp. sugar

1 tsp. vanilla

6 oz. cream cheese, at room temperature

¾ cup powdered sugar

CHOCOLATE TOPPING

¾ cup milk chocolate chips

1 Tbsp. butter

2 Tbsp. cream

BACON BROWNIES

Sprinkling the bacon and pecans on top of the brownies lets people know that this isn't a run-of-the-mill dessert; it's a luxurious dive into the world of bacon.

1. Preheat the oven to 350 degrees. Grease a 9 × 11 pan with nonstick cooking spray. Set aside.

2. In a medium-sized mixing bowl, combine the flour, cocoa powder, sugar, and salt. Add the butter, eggs, and vanilla. Beat well. Stir half the bacon and half the pecans into the batter by hand. Spread the batter into the prepared pan and sprinkle with the remaining bacon and pecans.

3. Bake for 30–35 minutes, or until a toothpick inserted near the center comes out with crumbs but not batter.

4. Melt the candy melts according to the package directions, and drizzle over the top of the brownies before they cool.

1 cup flour

¾ cup cocoa powder

2 cups sugar

½ tsp. salt

½ cup butter, melted

4 eggs

2 tsp. vanilla

1 (12-oz.) pkg. bacon, cooked and chopped, divided

1 cup pecan halves, divided

½ cup candy melts

 **BACON BITS**

Bacon comes in three basic thicknesses:

Thick	⅛ inch
Regular	¹⁄₁₆ inch
Thin	¹⁄₃₂ inch

EASY BACON CARAMELS

Makes 50 caramels

Don't be intimidated by the candy thermometer. Using one is a straight-forward process and this is a great recipe to try it out.

1. Prepare an 8 × 8 pan by buttering it liberally. Do not use nonstick cooking spray. Set aside.

2. In a medium-sized saucepan, bring the sugar and corn syrup to a boil over medium heat. Slowly add the cream, stirring as you go. Make sure the caramel continues to boil as you add the cream. This can take 3–5 minutes. Once the cream is stirred in, add the butter and stir until melted. Clip a candy thermometer onto the side of the pan and cook the caramel until it reaches 230 degrees.

3. Remove the pan from the heat and stir in the vanilla. Pour the caramel into the prepared pan and put in the fridge to set, about an hour.

4. Use the oven method (page xi) to cook the bacon, then use kitchen shears to cut it into 1-inch pieces. If you cut while it's still warm, it won't crumble as easily. Set aside.

5. Once the caramel has set, cut it into 1 inch squares. If it is too hard, allow it to sit at room temperature for 15–20 minutes before cutting. Set aside.

6. Melt the candy melts according to package directions. Use forks to dip the caramel into the chocolate. Place the candy on a piece of wax paper and top with a piece of bacon. Repeat with the remaining caramels and bacon.

1 cup sugar

1 cup dark corn syrup

1 cup heavy cream

¼ cup butter

1 tsp. vanilla

10 slices bacon

2 (12-oz.) pkg. milk chocolate candy melts

BACON AND CHOCOLATEY CHOCOLATE COOKIES

One of the reasons bacon has become so popular is that it can stand alone or match up with other flavors, like chocolate. These cookies are a decadent combination sure to bring a smile to your bacon-lovin' face.

1. Preheat the oven to 350 degrees.
2. Beat the butter, shortening, and sugar in a medium-sized mixing bowl until light and fluffy. Add the vanilla and eggs and beat again scraping down the sides of the bowl as needed.
3. Add the flour, cocoa powder, baking soda, and salt. Mix well.
4. Stir in the bacon, candy bars, and toffee bits by hand.
5. Measure out by rounded tablespoonful and roll into balls. Place 1 inch apart on an ungreased cookie sheet and bake for 8–10 minutes or until the cookies fall when the cookie sheet is slapped on the counter.

 **BACON BITS**

Bacon goes beyond breakfast (and lunch and dinner). Bacon lovers no longer need to restrict their bacon obsession to a plate. You can find bacon flavored gumballs, jelly beans, and even mints, online and in specialty stores. For the especially addicted, there's also bacon-flavored dental floss.

Makes 36 cookies

½ cup butter

½ cup shortening

1½ cups sugar

2 tsp. vanilla

2 eggs

1 cups flour

⅔ cup cocoa powder

1 tsp. baking soda

½ tsp. salt

6 slices bacon, cooked to a crisp and chopped

2 (1.55-oz.) milk chocolate candy bars, chopped

½ cup English toffee bits

BACON TRIFLE

For this recipe, your bacon should be crisp but not burnt. The oven cooking technique found on page xi is the best method for this recipe.

1. Cook the pudding according to package directions. Transfer to a cool bowl and set in the fridge for 10–15 minutes, or until it sets up and no longer runs when the bowl it tipped.

2. While the pudding is cooling, pour the cream into a medium-sized mixing bowl and beat it with a hand mixer until stiff peaks form. Add the vanilla and sugar. Set aside.

3. Cut the banana bread into 1-inch cubes. Set aside.

4. To create the layered look of a trifle, you're going to place half the bread cubes in the bottom of 6 clear glasses. Divide half the bacon between the glasses, then half the pudding, and then half the whipped cream. Repeat the process to create distinct layers, reserving a little of the bacon to sprinkle on top of the finished trifle.

1 (3.5-oz.) pkg. cook & serve butterscotch-flavored pudding

2 cups milk (or the amount called for on pudding package)

1½ cups whipping cream

1 tsp. vanilla

¼ cup sugar

1 large loaf banana bread

1 (12-oz.) pkg. bacon, cooked and crumbled

 **BACON BITS**

Bacon goes beyond breakfast (and lunch and dinner). Bacon lovers no longer need to restrict their bacon obsession to a plate. You can find bacon flavored gumballs, jelly beans, and even mints, online and in specialty stores. For the especially addicted, there's also bacon-flavored dental floss.

BACON S'MORES

The key to making a good bacon s'more is to have two layers of bacon—one just isn't enough. You'll want to move your oven rack down to the center position as indicated in the directions; otherwise your marshmallow will burn and your chocolate will melt too quickly.

1. Place the graham crackers on a cookie sheet. On one graham cracker, place the chocolate and two pieces of bacon. On the other graham cracker, place the remaining pieces of bacon and then the marshmallow on top.

2. Move your oven rack to the center position and turn your oven on to high broil. Put the cookie sheet in the oven and cook for 3–5 minutes, or until the marshmallow is lightly toasted and the chocolate is slightly melted.

3. Once it is ready, remove the cookie sheet and carefully press the marshmallow side gently into the chocolate side. Devour!

1 graham cracker, cut in half

1 marshmallow

½ a candy bar

2 slices bacon, cooked and cut in half

BACON TRUFFLES

Serves 12

If you're looking for a way to jazz up Father's Day, these truffles are the perfect touch. Hand Dad a box of these and watch his eyes light up.

1. In a medium-sized sauce pan, melt the chocolate chips, butter, and cream together until smooth, about 7 minutes. Stir in the bacon. Pour the mixture into a bowl and allow to cool in the fridge for about an hour.

2. Spread the potato chip crumbs out on a shallow plate.

3. Once the chocolate has cooled enough to hold its shape, use a teaspoon to measure out enough chocolate for a truffle. Roll the chocolate between your palms to make a ball. Roll the ball in the potato chip crumbs. Store covered in the fridge for up to five days, or eat immediately.

1 (11.5-oz.) pkg. milk chocolate chips

1 Tbsp. butter

3 Tbsp. cream

6 slices hickory smoked bacon, cooked to a crisp

1 cup crushed potato chips

COOKING MEASUREMENT EQUIVALENTS

Cups	Tablespoons	Fluid Ounces
⅛ cup	2 Tbsp.	1 fl. oz.
¼ cup	4 Tbsp.	2 fl. oz.
⅓ cup	5 Tbsp. + 1 tsp.	
½ cup	8 Tbsp.	4 fl. oz.
⅔ cup	10 Tbsp. + 2 tsp.	
¾ cup	12 Tbsp.	6 fl. oz.
1 cup	16 Tbsp.	8 fl. oz.

Cups	Fluid Ounces	Pints/Quarts/Gallons
1 cup	8 fl. oz.	½ pint
2 cups	16 fl. oz.	1 pint = ½ quart
3 cups	24 fl. oz.	1½ pints
4 cups	32 fl. oz.	2 pints = 1 quart
8 cups	64 fl. oz.	2 quarts = ½ gallon
16 cups	128 fl. oz.	4 quarts = 1 gallon

Other Helpful Equivalents

1 Tbsp.	3 tsp.
8 oz.	½ lb.
16 oz.	1 lb.

METRIC MEASUREMENT EQUIVALENTS

Approximate Weight Equivalents

Ounces	Pounds	Grams
4 oz.	¼ lb.	113 g
5 oz.		142 g
6 oz.		170 g
8 oz.	½ lb.	227 g
9 oz.		255 g
12 oz.	¾ lb.	340 g
16 oz.	1 lb.	454 g

Approximate Volume Equivalents

Cups	US Fluid Ounces	Milliliters
⅛ cup	1 fl. oz.	30 ml
¼ cup	2 fl. oz.	59 ml
½ cup	4 fl. oz.	118 ml
¾ cup	6 fl. oz.	177 ml
1 cup	8 fl. oz.	237 ml

Other Helpful Equivalents

½ tsp.	2½ ml
1 tsp.	5 ml
1 Tbsp.	15 ml

INDEX

ABOUT THE AUTHOR

Christina Dymock lives with her husba
and four children in a small town in Cen
Utah. A graduate from the University of Ut
she has had careers as an editor and adju
instructor at Salt Lake Community Colle
and an author. Besides her cookbooks, Ch
tina has been published in *Woman's We
Magazine* and several *Chicken Soup for the S*
books. When she's not in the kitchen or at
computer, she enjoys running, skiing, wa
boarding, sewing, and reading.